Power Publishing Secrets

The Email Marketing Blueprint for
Nonfiction Authors

Sharlrita DeLoatch

Copyright © 2024 Sharlrita DeLoatch
All rights reserved. No part of this book may be reproduced or used in any manner without the prior written permission of the copyright owner, except for the use of brief quotations in a book review.

Paperback ISBN: 979-8-9889181-2-7

To request permissions, contact the author at Sharlrita@SharlritaDeloatch.com

Published & Printed by:

BWE Publishing and Consulting
4501 New Bern Ave STE 130 Box 144
Raleigh, NC 27610
1800-652-5139

www.bwepublishingandconsulting.com

FREEBIE FOR MY AMAZING READERS

I have a special gift for my readers! I've created a workbook to compliment this book so that you can do the work to build your email list today!

Scan the QR code below to get access or visit https://powerpublishingsecrets.com/workbook2

Table of Contents

INTRODUCTION v

Chapter One The Secret Weapon For Subscriber Growth 1

Chapter Two The Gateway To Valuable Resources: Your Landing Page 5

Chapter Three Simple Tweaks, Big Results: Grow Your Email List Fast 8

Chapter Four Turn Viewers into Fans: Webinars for Subscriber Growth & Trust 14

Chapter Five Fast-Track Your Subscriber Growth: Facebook Strategies 18

Chapter Seven: Fast-Track Client Growth: Building Winning Partnerships 26

Chapter Eight Reach Thousands Of Potential Subscribers (Literally) Overnight 30

INTRODUCTION

Some people may say that email marketing is dead but on the other hand some people may say there is money on the email list. What do I say? I say every author needs to grow an email list way before they hit publish. If you are really serious you will grow your list while you are writing your book. From the dawn of the internet, building an email list has proven to be an important way to stay in touch with your customers, clients, and prospects. So, don't believe the naysayers...email marketing is alive and well.

In this book I am going to walk through some strategies that will assist you with adding new subscribers to your list in the next 30 days. I highly recommend completing all of them and I have crafted this book along with your worksheets so that each step builds upon the last.

However, don't get overwhelmed thinking you have to implement these all at once! Every one of these strategies works, both alone and in conjunction with the other methods, so begin with the strategy that resonates with you most, then branch off and try the other methods after your first opt-in is in place.

Just as you can make the most amount of money with multiple income streams, so can you attract more email subscribers by utilizing multiple methods.

You can count on your email list as a steady stream of income provided you build a targeted list and keep your books relevant to your audience. However, you must get started first with these strategies, so let's get started! I mentioned earlier that I did create some simple worksheets for you to go along with the book. You may download them at https://powerpublishingsecrets.com/workbook2

Chapter One

The Secret Weapon For Subscriber Growth

It is wishful thinking that your website visitors will remember your URL once they leave your site is NOT how to market your business! How frequently have you walked into a room and forgotten why? I have so many times and I thought it was because I was getting old. With all of the internet's distractions, do NOT rely on people to remember you.

Instead, give your web visitors a reason to leave their email addresses with you to stay in touch. Once they grant you permission to contact them again, you can customize your offers and make more sales. The more you stay in touch with your email list, the more your audience will know, like, and trust you, thereby increasing your sales and overall revenue.

I personally have an email newsletter where I send 3 quick and valuable resource Monday -Friday. That's my #1 way to grow my email list. Having a minimalist newsletter is what my bestie [Jamie Northrup](#) calls it allows me to not only stay in touch with my besties on a daily basis but also they hear from me daily not just when I am selling something. You can join my newsletter Elevate your digital publishing business daily at https://www.sharlritadeloatch.com/newsletter

First, sign up with an email marketing provider. Gmail or Yahoo Mail isn't a professional look, and those platforms won't allow you to email many hundreds or thousands of people at once; instead, you'll become known as a spammer and your email account may become disabled. I personally use [Convertkit](). It's easy to set up and you can start for FREE. I recorded a YouTube video on how to set up Convertkit if you choose to use them. Check it out https://youtu.be/rfyGOoy2WoQ?si=x_fzlJ9Xbp5MTv7n

I know you want to keep reading so along with the free workbook I will also have a resources section with the workbook for easy access. Let's get back to email providers...

Research email providers that allow tagging and look at their autoresponder options. Tagging is a simple way to segment your list based upon their interests in your business. If you offer an array of services or programs, you can tag customers based on what they purchased OR which opt-in they claimed.

An autoresponder allows you to schedule prewritten emails to be delivered at certain intervals. This option is especially useful if you want to offer an ecourse or if you offer evergreen information to your audience.

After you're signed up, it's time to brainstorm your opt-in offer. What value can you offer people to before they hand over their email address? Take some time to think this offer through because simply saying, "Sign up for my newsletter" or "Get my updates" are not enough to warrant interest in joining your list. You need to attract the **RIGHT people** to your list, so customize your offer to the type of person you want to serve.

Most importantly, think about how you can solve a specific problem with a short piece of content and provide your ideal clients with a quick win. Most frequently these offers are in the form of an eBook, but you can certainly offer audio, a checklist, or templates. More important than your format is the solution you're offering. Identify your audience's struggle, supply 3-5 tips for resolving that struggle, and you'll attract subscribers who are hungry for more answers.

Keep in mind, you're not giving away all your trade secrets. Your 3-5 tips are simply a glimpse of what your book offers. It's a way to bring new people into your circle of influence and woo them into your programs or into your private coaching calendar with your expertise.

Chapter Two

The Gateway To Valuable Resources: Your Landing Page

Now that you know what you're offering, it's time to figure out how to get people opting-in to get it. To do this, you'll need a simple landing page, as well as enticing copy to reel in new subscribers.

First, search your WordPress theme for a landing page template. If you have one built into your theme and you like the layout, then move onto writing compelling copy.

If you don't have a landing page template, then research platforms like Lead Pages or Click Funnels. Convertkit has some nice landing pages as well if you desire to keep everything in one place. How ever both Lead page and Click Funnels can create attractive, eye-catching landing pages with a drag-and-drop interface and built-in templates. Both platforms also have split testing capabilities, so you can test different versions of your landing page to see which one converts more views into sales.

Another option is to check with your email service provider if they have landing page capabilities. If so, then there's no worry about integration with your autoresponder. Start playing around with the design elements so you feel comfortable creating your page. If you decide to use Convertkit & Leadpages pages together I've created a quick video about how to get them to work together. You can check out the video <u>HERE</u>. I will also add the link to the resource page of the workbook.

One note: You need an opt-in box on this landing page, so be sure if you're using another landing page builder that they integrate seamlessly with your email provider.

Also, don't be afraid to use images on your landing page. Gone are the days of boring pages filled with miles of sales copy. Images help break up long copy and adds interest to your page. Consider adding a box all about YOU so new visitors can get a glimpse of who you are and why they should give you, their email.

Of course, with this being a free opt-in offer, you really don't want miles of sales copy. Keep your description short and sweet. Identify the problem(s) your audience is dealing with and a quick synopsis of how you're giving them the answers in this free gift.

Chapter Three

Simple Tweaks, Big Results: Grow Your Email List Fast

You already have a website, but is it working for you around-the-clock to bring in new subscribers? It could—and should—be! Gone are the days of boring old websites that serve as business cards on the web. It's time to up the ante on your current website and accelerate your growth. You can also easily add your opt-in to several other places on your site to ensure nobody misses out.

No matter which of these options you choose, you'll want them to be similar to your landing page: You'll need a headline, short description, opt-in form and call to action button.

Option #1: A pop-up opt-in form
You've seen these pop-ups: You're visiting a site and then like magic, a special offer appears. These pop-ups are attention-grabbing and have great conversions, depending on the relevance of your offer, of course.

This is one of the most popular and effective techniques and is offered by many email service providers. You can also use your choice of WordPress plugins for this option or use Leadpages but research the plugins carefully for ease of use and integration with your email service provider. As always, free plugins will have limited features as opposed to their paid versions, so consider that as well. Below is an example of a pop up on my website taking visitors to my Email Newsletter.

Option #2: Header opt-in form
Your website design and copy that appears "above the fold" – or before you have to start scrolling – is what will grab your visitors' attention first; therefore, make the best use of that space to draw subscribers to your free offer.

One such way is to build an opt-in box into your website header. There's no scrolling or guessing as to what to do next: Sign up for your list.

Option #3: Header opt-in plugin
If you want something more subtle – and easier to implement yourself onto your site – try using the HelloBar plugin for WordPress. This premium plugin inserts a bar across the very top of your website with your opt-in offer. It's subtle but is among the first things your new visitors will see so

it's effective. Amy is a great example of this using her podcast as an opt in opportunity.

Option #4: Below blog posts
So, you write a new blog post and you're publicizing it on social media. You're directing tons of traffic to your blog post but most of these people are new visitors. What do you want them to do AFTER they read your post?

Your answer should be: I want them to sign up to my list. Make that abundantly clear by inserting a simple opt-in at the end of each blog post. These visitors want the blog post first (that's why they clicked on your link in the first place) so they probably weren't ready to sign up when they saw your header opt-in. Capture them at the end of the post so you don't lose them forever.

To implement this option, you can create your opt-ins with your email service provider OR research WordPress plugins (such as Optin Forms). In both cases, you'll have to insert code at the end of each blog post, but the plugins generally use short codes which are easier to find in your WordPress dashboard than from your email provider.

Option #5: In the footer

Remember, you're making the most of your internet real estate and you never know when someone will actually scroll all the way down to your footer! Utilize this space with an opt-in form! Again, use either your email service provider code or a plugin that integrates easily with your email provider.

Option #6: Link in the main navigation menu
Even though this may seem like double duty if you also have a header opt-in, this is a smart move for those who enter your site via somewhere other than your home page (which is most likely where your header opt-in is located). Your navigation menu is visible on ALL your pages, so no matter where your visitor comes in, they will see your opt-in offer.

Pro note: Don't call it an "opt-in" or "freebie." That doesn't entice your visitors to click. Use the title (if it fits) or "Special Offer" or "Limited Time Offer" instead.

Option #7: Sidebar banner

Sidebars in WordPress were designed to house numerous widgets for ads and product endorsements. However, sidebars are often overlooked by those with internet experience, so don't rely completely on this placement to grow your list.

Pro tip: Start with one of these options and get it implemented; then track your results before adding another opt-in to another location.

Also, consider changing up the text if you want to implement more than one location OR insert different offers in each location once you have a process set for creating these opt-in offers.

Chapter Four

Turn Viewers into Fans: Webinars for Subscriber Growth & Trust

Let's step away from the opt-ins for a moment and explore how free webinars or workshops can explode your list as well.

People love video because this medium is the closest thing to seeing you in person. Your audience members don't have to travel or leave the comfort of their home to see you in action. They will see your face, hear your voice, and learn about your coaching style. Couple all those things with a powerful message, and you'll have people eating out of the palm of your hand in no time.

With free or paid webinars, you ask for registration ahead of time – similar to taking a head count or reserving their seats – because not all webinar platforms are the same in terms of the number of attendees allowed. So, you're presenting a fabulous webinar topic and directing those interested to a webinar registration page (landing page) where they will enter their email address to receive reminders as the date gets closer and to also receive the replay link.

NOTE: Most webinar platforms include these landing page features. However, if you prefer to have more control and ownership of your subscribers, set up a regular landing page in Leadpages or on your site, complete with your opt-in box. Write a sexy headline, describe the purpose of your webinar, and start sending traffic to that page. Set up an autoresponder series of webinar reminders so they are sent automatically.

Webinar attendees are often more motivated to do the work and implement the tips you discuss in the webinar because they are willing to give up an hour of their time to hear you speak. You're speaking to their pain points and offering a solution, so you have their undivided attention. They don't want that time wasted so be sure to deliver actionable tips they can follow immediately.

Allowing them to interact with you in real time is not only one of the fastest ways to build know, like and trust factor with your audience—it's also super valuable for them because they're more likely to actually do the work and get the quick win. Also remember that once the live webinar is recorded, it's very easy to set that up as an on-demand evergreen webinar that you can continue promoting year-round.

What you need for a webinar:

- ✓ Great topic ideas that speak to your audience's pain points. Make these DIFFERENT from your website opt-in so you can attract more people into your circle of influence. Think about the call to action at the end; attendees have already given you their email addresses upon registration so

think of a paid offer – either your own or an affiliate offer – and don't be shy about making that offer at the end of the webinar.
- ✓ A webinar platform, such as Zoom, GoToWebinar, or Livestorm. You'll find a hundred other options, so do your research and compare features. I personally use zoom. How many attendees will you attract? Check for recording options. If there's a trial available, check out the dashboard for ease of use. Be sure there's a way to integrate your webinar room with your email provider so those registration emails aren't "stuck" inside the webinar platform with no way to export them.
- ✓ If you're interested in running "on demand" evergreen webinars, check out platforms such as EverWebinar or StealthSeminar. Check out the items mentioned above along with the price tag. With the number of webinar platforms available, you'll find one that suits your budget.

Remember, people will spend money with you if they know, like, and trust you; so, if appearing on a webinar makes your palms sweat, bite that bullet and get your face in front of your audience. Those who NEED to hear your message will find you.

Chapter Five

Fast-Track Your Subscriber Growth: Facebook Strategies

Social media is an obvious–and easy–way to add new subscribers to your list. Facebook now give you an option to turn your personal page into a business page and it actually offers quite a few easy-yet-effective ways to grow your subscriber count.

Option #1: Add opt-in to your business profile.

What better way to attract attention than to set your Cover Art with a photo of your free offer linked to the product's opt-in page! Check out your email provider's integrations capabilities as each provider will have different instructions for integrating with Facebook. I placed an example of my Facebook Profile.

Option #2: Create a Facebook lead ad.

Lead ads are set up similarly to other ads that redirect to a landing page; however, when your prospect clicks your ad, a pre-populated form appears, making it very simple to enter their email without ever leaving the Facebook platform.

Go to your Facebook Ads Manager to begin creating your ad but choose Lead Generation as your objective.

Option #3: Add your opt-in to the Tabs section.

Consider your Facebook business page an extension of your website. From this one page you can add as much information as you have on your website and people don't have to leave Facebook to visit.

Go to your Facebook page and click the Settings tab. Next, click the Templates and Tabs link in the left margin and choose your template; the Services template will work for most coaches.

After that, you can choose which tabs to incorporate on your page. After you have chosen your Tabs, go back to your page and click the individual tab link in the left margin. Here is where you can customize your offers and redirect visitors back to your subscription or webinar landing pages. Your subscription opt-in can be a one-time change but if you're offering live webinars, be sure to update those whenever you have a new one to promote.

Option #4: Edit your short bio on your Facebook business page.

Add your link to your bio to redirect to your freebie's landing page. Again, use a strong phrase to catch people's attention instead of just "Subscribe."

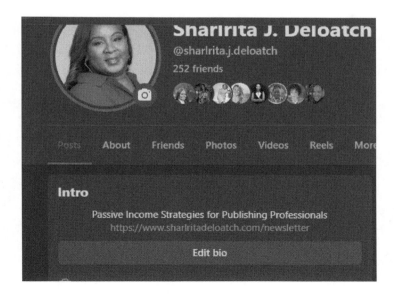

Chapter Six
Instagram Subscriber Magnet: Design & Promote Your Opt-In

Instagram isn't new on the scene, but it has become more and more popular with business owners and coaches over the years. The good news: There are almost as many ways to direct people to your mailing list right from your IG page as there are cute photos to scroll through. You can use your IG profile, IG stories and even IG highlights to add subscribers.

Option #1: Change your "link in bio" to your freebie URL or make sure that your link in bio as the link to your email list.

Your link in bio is the clickable URL that visitors click on to learn more about you from your Instagram profile. This link can easily be customized to link to your opt-in freebie or webinar landing page.

Option #2: Create a post and/or Story all about your freebie.

You should have a beautiful product graphic for your freebie so start sharing that with the world! With your Story, utilize the "links" feature to send them to your landing page. With a regular post, connect with your audience so they want to find your link in bio to sign up. You've worked hard on this opt-in offer; don't be afraid to share it.

Option #3: Consider alternative ways to get people on your list from Instagram.

Keep talking up your free offer but instead of relying only on your link in bio, try asking your followers to comment on your post and you can use automations such as manychat. When they comment a keyword you set they will automatically be sent the landing page for your freebie. That's neat right?

Option #4: Create lead ads for Instagram.

In case you didn't know, Facebook owns Instagram so you can utilize the lead ads process in the same way for Facebook. First, create your Facebook business page AND an Instagram business profile. When you have both, login to the Facebook Ads Manager and create your lead ads.

Option #5: Go Live on Instagram

Much like Facebook Lives, Instagram allows you to chat with your audience live with a simple click of a button. Talk up your freebie offer. Encourage engagement with your viewers. Announce your Lives in advance to build buzz and tell them during the live about your freebie.

Option #6: Takeover a JV partner's Instagram Story.

This method can be fun if you have a plan of action AND a supportive JV partner who believes in your offer. The takeover generally involves a lower-level brand taking over a more well-known brand for a certain period of time. During that time, the newer brand makes Story posts to further their reach and to promote their freebie offer. It's another way to tap into someone else's market, provided you have strong content to offer.

Let your creativity soar and have fun! Stick with what works and ditch the methods that don't yield results.

Chapter Seven:

Fast-Track Client Growth: Building Winning Partnerships

It's all well and good to dangle your mailing list in front of people who already know, like and trust you—but partnerships and other Joint Ventures are an incredibly effective way to find NEW ideal clients and subscribers hungry for what you have.

Like anything else in marketing, you need to make a concerted effort to market yourself and your business. We're not in the "hoping people will find me" business; we're in the "I solve problems for people and I'm awesome" business!

First, think of people you admire who have a similar market that you would like to reach. How can you help their audiences? How can you prove your worth to these inspiring people who are very protective of their subscribers?

Understanding your own message is a key point. Know what problems you're solving. What is your superpower and how will you appeal to these new audience members? You'll have to prove yourself in your pitch that you're not just out to poach subscribers or customers. Prove that you have an authentic desire to help others and be sure YOUR message is on point with the JV's audience. You're only wasting everyone's time if you're not targeting JVs with similar demographics and messages.

Also, aim BIG for the biggest impact. Want to be on Ellen's show or the Today Show? Landing one of those gigs will bring you traffic for years and that's how you should consider how to make JV pitches. Smaller business owners can also become your biggest affiliates but having a mix of bigger and smaller is important so you're not putting all your eggs in one basket.

When you're doing research, keep a spreadsheet to stay organized with potential names, URLs, and contact info. Also include the dates and number of times you reached out to these JV prospects. If you're hearing crickets after two or three attempts, move on to the next name. Also set yourself a goal to reach out to a certain number of people each day or week. You may not have control over who wants to partner with you, but you DO have control of how much energy you put into finding those partners.

Lastly, make each pitch personal. Even if you start off with a general template for a JV pitch email, really make changes for each recipient. Have you done your research on each JV prospect? Do you know anything about their business? If they have a podcast or YouTube channel, have you listened or watched to know what they talk about? Are you sure your markets are a fit? Lazy JV pitches will get tossed and potentially ruin reputations. Put your best foot forward by doing your research.

Another fun way to gain subscribers is to run a giveaway or contest using your favorite social media platform (be sure to check their terms of service first, so you're following all the rules properly). Choose something fun and exciting that your subscribers WANT, set the rules for the giveaway, and then keep promoting the contest to drive traffic to your social platform or a landing page where contestants can enter their email address.

It's not enough, however, to promote the contest once and then sit back and wait. Interact with these new subscribers both on social media and via emails. Prove to them that you have great content to share and build up lots of buzz for when you choose the winner of the giveaway.

Chapter Eight

Reach Thousands Of Potential Subscribers (Literally) Overnight

Organic traffic is amazing, and you should always optimize your website, so the search engines consistently bring new visitors to your website. However, paid ads are another way to increase your reach if you're ready to put a little cash in the game.

If your opt-in has proven successful with minimal promotion within your social circles, consider running paid ads on Facebook and/or Instagram. The good news is you already have (almost) everything you need—and most of the time, the leads you receive from paid advertising are people you wouldn't have been able to reach otherwise.

First, decide which opt-in you'd like to run an ad to. Do you have a freebie PDF, upcoming live webinar, or automated on-demand webinar? Direct your ads to one of those landing pages to gather email addresses.

Second, decide how much money you want to spend on this campaign. You can set a daily budget or a total budget; when the campaign meets its maximum, your ad campaign will stop.

Third, choose your demographics. Knowing your target market is imperative to gaining the most ROI from this advertising effort. What's the point of showing your ads to a million people if 999,000 of them don't care about what you have to offer? Don't be afraid to drill down deep to reach your target audience. Those are the people who will purchase your services or products.

Fourth, write a captivating and sexy headline. Headlines are what capture attention first so go bold and don't settle for boring.

Fifth, write your ad copy. Again, make it exciting and work to entice your audience to keep reading. Play to their pain points and struggles. Talk about your own story and how you can relate to your audience. Reassure them that you have the answer they've been searching for.

Lastly, choose an image that is eye-catching to draw your audience in. Make a purchase from a stock photo house but make sure the photo also makes sense coupled with your copy. If your audience senses a disconnect between the two, they'll lose faith that you have the answers.

Once your ad campaign begins, visit your insights page in your ad manager dashboard. You'll see the number of impressions and how many people have seen your ad. You can also check your email provider to see how many have actually signed up for your offer during the campaign timeframe. Take these notes and use them to plan your next campaign and make tweaks to improve your overall ad performance.

To make tracking easier, consider creating an individual landing page for each ad campaign. That way you can still promote your offer while the campaign is running but you'll have distinct data about how your ad converted to opt-ins. The landing pages would look identical except for the URL.

If you don't want to invest in ads you can check out this website called Udimi

This is where you can partner with people who already have a large following and you pay a small amount to advertise. I plan to use Udimi and will document my findings and results on Youtube so make sure you are subscribed to my YouTube channel

There you have it! A total breakdown on how you can gain 1000 subscribers on your email list in 30 days. You can do this just stay consistent in your list building efforts. There is money on the list, but you have to build it first.

Get Your Book Writing & Publishing Started

Scan the code and access the Self-Publishing Toolkit today

About the Author

Hello, I'm Sharlrita Deloatch, a resident of Raleigh, NC. I am blessed with a wonderful husband, Anthony, and my fabulous seven children (four of whom I gave birth to, LOL). As an author, I specialize in creating books that teach publishers and writers how to monetize their writing skills by teaching 40 effective strategies for publishing, digital marketing, and leveraging online platforms. I am deeply committed to nurturing my Youtube Family and providing value to my community through my complimentary email newsletter, Elevate your Digital Publishing Business Daily. I invite all writers, creatives and publishers to become part of my newsletter. I am dedicated to continually delivering value and support to my amazing readers! Please feel free to reach out to me if you have any questions or concerns. You can find my contact information in any of my books. Sending big hugs and love,

Sharlrita DeLoatch

Email: Sharlrita@SharlritaDeloatch.com

Need 1:1 consulting? Book a call at https://www.chatwithsharlrita.com/

Made in United States
Orlando, FL
30 December 2024